UKRAINE 300 to 2014

A short history

Anthony Clayton

Note

Names of individuals and places that figure in this work are recorded in modern Ukrainian form with names used in previous history writing following in brackets. An exception is made for the Tsars of Russia where customary anglophone nomenclature is retained

Preface

Ukraine, a part of the world that had not figured on the world stage since the Second World War has suddenly appeared as a scene of violent conflict. This short work sets out to summarise the deep historical roots of the present strife for the benefit of many who have a concern for Ukraine.

Acknowledgments

Its production has been possible thanks to a number of friends. For the provision of factual material my thanks go to Michael Benjamin and to Andrew Orgill and his staff at the library of the Royal Military Academy, Sandhurst. Without the help of John Card in the technical production and Julie Card in converting my manuscript – with all its difficult names – into typescript, this work could never have appeared. I am very grateful.

Anthony Clayton
Farnham
Surrey
UK
July 2014

Contents

Introduction i

Map of Ukraine (present day) iii

Chapter 1 From Byzantium to the Polish-Lithuanian Union 1

Chapter 2 Russia and Ukraine 9

Chapter 3 Catherine the Great and "New Russia" 13

Chapter 4 The Nineteenth Century and Pre 1914 Years 17

Chapter 5 The First World War and its Aftermath 23

Chapter 6 Communist Ukraine 1920-1941 27

Chapter 7 The Second World War 1941-1945 31

Chapter 8 The Soviet Union 1945-1991 35

Chapter 9 Independent Ukraine 1991-2014 41

Introduction

The word Ukraine means frontier or border land. The country is a border land which has been fought over by several powerful neighbours who intervened and colonised. One of these, for long Ukraine's northern neighbour, Poland, was herself situated between powerful rivals but nevertheless was able to develop a nation, a language, a culture and a strong sense of national identity. Ukraine was never able to do this as successive waves of migrants of very different cultures followed each other in invasions. The flat steppes country provided no natural obstacles to such invasions and, apart from the Black Sea, no natural frontiers. But the Steppes also provide a rich breadbasket for very large grain exports. For long the region was referred to as "The Black Sea Steppes" or "the Ukraine", geographic rather than national labels and there remain very wide differences of identity held by inhabitants of Ukraine on what it means to be a Ukrainian. For some it is a hope for a totally independent liberal sovereign state, for others a return to past unions with Russia, for others a federal Ukraine in which the regions' peoples could live and be governed within the culture of their choice, Ukrainian or Russian, and yet others scarred by the experience of living memory, indifference so long as the social order is stable. This work, then, is about an area of the earth's surface stretching between Lviv in the north west, along the north shores of the Black Sea as far as Mariupol, and the different peoples that have lived in this area, a number no longer doing so. The reasons for the presence of these peoples, now and in the past, is the history of Ukraine.

Ukraine (present day)

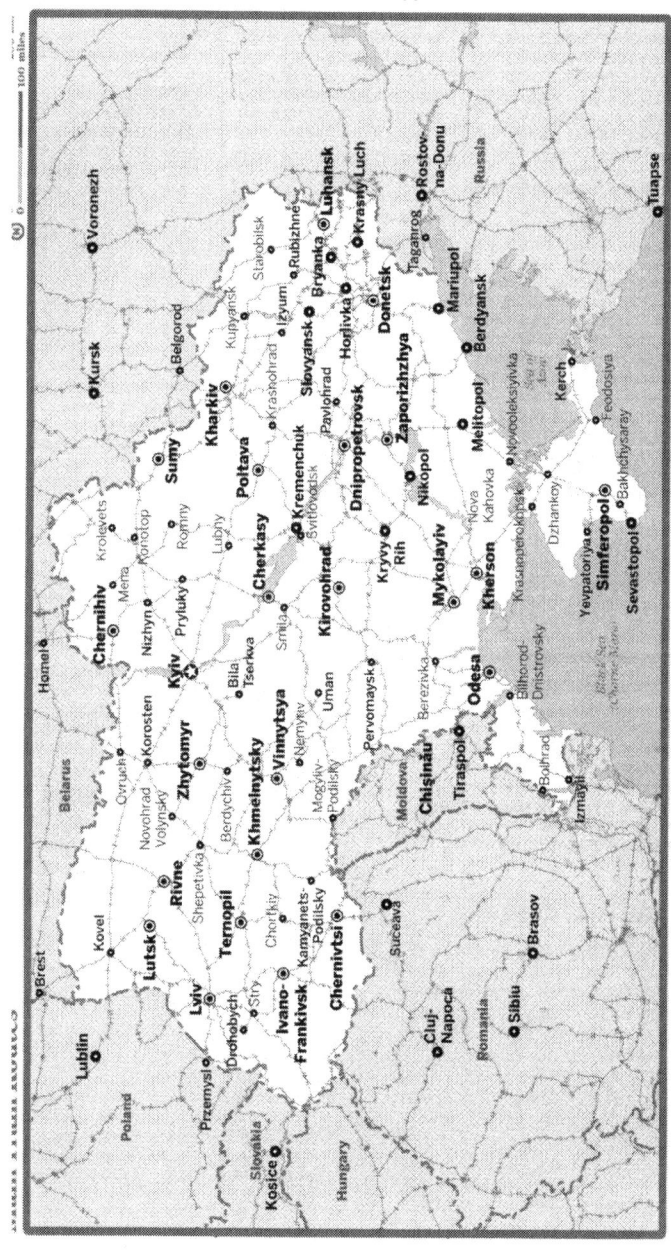

Reproduced with permission from Ukraine 4, Marc Di Duca et al. © 2014 Lonely Planet

Chapter 1 From Byzantium to the Polish-Lithuanian Union

A kingdom of a nomad people, the Scythians inhabited most of what we now know as Ukraine some 600 years before Christ; they traded with Greeks and later Romans in search of corn. A small settlement and port was established in the Crimea. The Romans called Crimea Taurida, as its shape to them appeared to resemble that of a bull.

The first of the long series of incursions into Europe by successive waves of Asian peoples occurred in the 1st Century AD. These were Slavs, many red-haired, who moved down from Moscow and the Minsk areas along the Dnieper river, others entered via Romania and Moldova. These were followed in the late 4th Century by Goths, who also entered from the south-west and in so doing beginning the severing of contacts between the Western Roman Empire and the Black Sea region. Other peoples, notably one ethnicity referred to as "Bulgars" by later chroniclers followed, and in the early 5th Century the Huns swept across north Black Sea coast region creating chaos.

Faced with these incursions and the severing of contacts, the Roman Empire had begun to split. Under the Emperor Diocletian in 293 arrangements were made for two Empires, the Emperor at Byzantium on the European side of the Bosphorus being the senior. The division was to be administrative but cultural divisions were soon to follow. Even within the administrations feuding was also to follow, to be ended in the second and third decades of the 4th Century by Constantine who secured control over both empires. In honour of this achievement Byzantium was confirmed as the capital and renamed Constantinople, a name to last until the early 1920s. The city's strategic and commercial importance was highlighted by a Persian army menacing Anatolia, an additional reason for the emperor's choice, but the empire saw the Danube as its northern frontier. Ukraine was a borderland beyond this frontier. A trading port, to be fortified later was established at Cherson, near the present-day Sevastopol on the Crimean peninsula; it combined defence, intelligence collection, missionary activity and trade for many years. Inland, further north, according to handed down oral history the city of Kyiv was founded in the 5th Century by a Slav prince.

The second development of major far-reaching importance was the declaration by Constantine at the time that he was securing control that he had become a Christian; his followers were then expected to convert. Christianity at that time was far from united, bishoprics within the empire holding divergent views centring on the natures of Christ and the Holy Spirit. Greek was the language of the Church in the East, Latin the language of the West. Successive Councils within the empire argued and debated on issues both abstract and practical. Full formal division was to follow later in 1054 over two issues. The first was theological, the Western Church asserting that the Holy Spirit was descended from both the Father and the Son, the Eastern Church stating that the Holy Spirit was descended from the Father only. The second issue was over Church administration, in particular over the primacy of the Pope of Rome. Mainstream Greek and later Russian Churches in loose federations have followed the Eastern traditions. Later in the 16th Century Uniat Churches appeared in Ukraine and the Minsk-Smolensk areas of Russia now called Belarus. These were, and still are essentially Roman Catholic in teaching and faith with full communion with Rome, but with their own canon law and liturgies. Priests are allowed to marry and have families.

In the 7th Century Crimea became involved in one of the endless dynastic disputes. The Emperor Justinian II was overthrown in 692 by a Byzantine nobles' coup. His nose was split open and he was exiled to Crimea. From there, and with the aid of the local "Bulgar" khan he launched a counter-attack and recaptured Constantinople. But the "Bulgars" and the khan turned against him and in 711 he was overthrown and beheaded.

In this time fresh ethnic invasions were increasing and save for a few Byzantine interventions Crimea and all Ukraine became cut off from Byzantium. Beginning in 862 the Pechenegs swept in pushing the small Slav communities northwards towards Moscow and the land was reduced to chaos. Some order in the Kyiv area was restored with the appearance on the scene of fresh invaders from the north, the Varangians, a people of Swedish origin. Under prince Oleh's rule from 889 the foundations of "Kievan Rus" were laid later to assert a measure of authority from northern Russia to the Danube under princes of the Rurik dynasty in a loose confederation of small principalities. In 989 the most important of the Varangians, Volodymyr the Great, with an eye to Dnieper river trade with the empire married Anna, the sister of the Byzantine Emperor Basil II. He converted to Christianity, his people obediently following him with a mass baptism in the Dnieper. Later Volodymyr set out for Moscow taking with him Eastern Church theology, rituals and organisation. Missionaries from Byzantium arrived in Kyiv. Churches and monasteries were built, the cathedral of St Sophia, planned to have thirteen domes was begun in 1097. Volodymyr's son, Yaroslav the Wise extended the fame of Kievan Rus far and wide and making it the largest country in Europe. For a while the security of Kievan Rus was maintained by a chain of forts protecting Kyiv against Pecheneg attacks from the south, the Byzantines holding most of the Crimea and the conversion to Christianity of other Varangians and the Slav rural peoples to the north. In 1018 in the course of a war with Poland the Polish king Boleslas the Brave entered Kyiv in triumph but his interests were limited to influence and trade and he sought no territorial gain, his incursion though marks the first of many Polish invasions later.

In the late 11th and 12th Centuries the power and influence of Byzantium had weakened. The Turkic "Bulgars" were being pushed eastwards by other Turks, "Khazars" or Cossacks, the Pechenegs still a menace in central Ukraine; and a new Asian people, the Polovtsi, also pushed from behind by the Turks, sweeping in from the east sacking Kyiv in one raid. Galicia and Volhynia however survived under a strong local dynasty until the 1330s. Seriously weakened central Kievan Rus was just able to survive until 1240 when the new and massive waves of Tartar and Mongol hordes poured down on all of eastern Europe. The son of Genghis Khan, Ogadei, was elected Great Khan in 1239 continuing the moves into eastern Europe but on his death faction fighting broke out among members of the family, conflicts which even the powerful Kubilai could not control. Kyiv was sacked by another son of Genghis, Batu, in 1240. In the same year Ukraine and Crimea were taken by the Khanate of The Golden Horde (Region) whose other strongholds also soon fell apart, leaving central Ukraine for long in the hands of the local Khan of Crimea. Kyiv and other smaller Slav rural communities were tolerated, though periodically raided. In 1333 in a final Mongol and Tartar sweep Volhynia and Galicia in the west were overrun but were checked by a military victory won by the King of Lithuania Gedymin, who nevertheless recognised his own limits far from home, an ally was needed.

In 1330 one of the greatest monarchs of mediaeval Europe, Casimir III came to the throne of Poland. His achievements and reforms in Poland, including the founding of the famous Kraków University must lie outside this work but he believed in the recovery of Volhynia and Galicia and a Polish annexation. He recovered Galicia in 1349 but a repulse at the hands of the Lithuanians necessitated a second campaign which in 1352 secured the western areas of Volhynia though Gedymin and his successors remained in control at Kyiv. The frontiers of Poland including Lviv were thereby outlined – to last until 1918. Casimir saw that the future stability of the area must rest on a Polish-Lithuanian partnership. Casimir died with no direct heir but his aim was carried forward by the Union of Krewo with the marriage of his niece, Jadwiga to Jagiello, King of Lithuania and grandson of Gedymin in 1386. The marriage had been delayed by an urgent political need for a campaign to subdue a new threat, that of local Russian chieftains and clans in the Lviv area and Jadwiga's reluctance to marry Jagiello, her preference being a Polish Masovian prince. For the Lithuanians the need for an alliance with Poland was reaffirmed after a severe Lithuanian defeat at the hands of the Tartars in 1399, the menace of the Teutonic Knights on the Baltic shore and the new threat of Russian designs after the ending of the civil strife in Muscovy.

The foundations not only of Polish rule but the whole Polish order in what was five hundred years later to become part of a Ukraine polity were now set in place. Landowners, mostly Polish but some Hungarian, German or Lithuanian who soon adopted the Polish language and if not already so became Roman Catholic, developed large estates with peasant or serf labour. Lviv became a Polish city, the language of administration and law became Polish. Lithuanian and Polish nobles settled increasingly in north Ukraine. The Uniat Church with its compromise teachings was created later in 1596 in the hope that this would end any remaining loyalties to the Patriarchs of Moscow and Constantinople but a number of the region's notables became Roman Catholics for their own advantage. The Uniat Church, or more correctly the several Uniat Churches came to have the reverse effect of that intended. The open dislike and arrogance of the Polish Roman Catholic hierarchy drove the Uniat into becoming the vanguard of Ukrainian proto nationalism, rebelling against the Polish establishment.

The Polish-Lithuanian union was briefly strengthened by a combination of forces, which even included a Tartar contingent, in the great defeat of the Teutonic Knights at the battle of Tannenberg in 1410. But dissension and fighting among the Lithuanians followed in the 1420s and by the time of Jagiello's death in 1434 the union was in decline, the Poles twice firmly rejecting Lithuanian claims for Lviv.

Elsewhere the last Asian invasion as powerful as any of the previous waves was that of the Moslem Ottoman Turks advancing into the Byzantine empire, reaching its ultimate triumph in the fall of Constantinople in 1453. The Khanate of the Crimea, which had had good relations with Poland, was overthrown by the Ottomans who destroyed the Khan's authority, reducing him to a vassal of the Sultan and occupying a small Genoese town, Kaffa, on the Crimean peninsula. Ottoman rule now extended along the coast as far as the Sea of Azov.

In 1556 the Ottomans conquered the Khanate of Astrakhan, bringing the Turkic peoples to the Volga, to form the future small self-governing Volga statelets that exist to this day. Moscow's ruler, Ivan IV "the Terrible" subjugated the Don Cossacks. The Dnieper Zaporag Cossacks supposedly subject to the Lithuanian crown remained largely uncontrolled dwelling in colonies on islands in the Dnieper and living on plunder, mounting raids as far afield as Constantinople in defiance of the Sultan. The Cossacks by this time had become and were for long to remain, communities of horsed outlaw adventurers, electing their own leaders and living in a defended stronghold know as the Sich

Amid the frequent quarrels over Baltic and north Polish issues a treaty was with difficulty agreed at Lublin in 1569 creating a Polish-Lithuanian Commonwealth in which all the small communities in central Ukraine including Kyiv were to pass to the crown of Poland. Authority and control was to follow in the late 1570s when the Polish King, Stephen Bathory subjugated the region, organising a number of the communities into Cossack and Slav self-defence militias while at the same time the Kyiv area was protected by a series of defensive earthworks which gave the city some protection against raiding. The Cossack chieftains who had cooperated with Stephen, though, very soon found Polish rule oppressive, particularly when supported by the Jesuits; important consequences for Ukraine were to follow.

One other very different late 15th – early 16th Centuries' move of peoples needs mention. The Ashkenazi branch of the Jewish peoples were driven out of several German principalities in the Holy Roman Empire, Poland and Lithuania. They settled in what became known as the "Jewish Pale", inland from the north western coast of the Black Sea, Moldova in present day terms with some also in regions later to be Ukrainian.

Chapter 2 Russia and Ukraine

The 17th Century was to see the arrival on the scene of the lead player to dominate the future of Ukraine in one form or another, Russia. Moscow, from 1598 to 1618 suffered a long period of dynastic in-fighting following Ivan the Terrible's murder of his son. Claims by pretenders only ended with the arrival on the throne of the first Tsar of the Romanov dynasty, Michael whose early years were preoccupied with the Polish War and their occupation of Moscow. At an apparent peak of their power the Poles supported Cossack raids as far south as the Ottoman Black Sea shores and an uprising in Moldova, but in 1618 they were forced to withdraw from Moscow. In an agreement with Michael they renounced their claim to rule in Moscow but were able to gain Kyiv and territory in Ukraine across the Dnieper. A war with the Ottomans and a Tartar revolt led to a serious Polish military defeat in 1620 which temporarily cost Poland control of the Black Sea coast. A year later the Poles were victorious and after final operations against the Russians, Polish authority over most of Ukraine was restored with revolts in 1636 and 1638 being suppressed.

Of much longer term significance was the appearance on the scene in 1648 of a man whom some but by no means all Ukrainians were later to rebrand as a founder of Ukrainian nationalism. By birth a Pole, Bohdan Khmelnytsky (Bogdan Chmielnicki) owner of a small estate had been victimised by a noble of the Lviv area establishment who had killed his son and sacked his estate. In revenge, supported by peasant Cossacks and Tartars across Volhynia and Podolia, he led an exceedingly bloody uprising defeating the Polish army with the aid of Tartar cavalry in a battle at Pyliavtsi and slaughtering Polish nobles and their families, Jews, Roman and Uniat priests, usually after torture. The townsmen of Lviv were able to safeguard their city and a Polish army won two victories in battle with Khmelnytsky, first a small-scale success in defence of a small town Zbaraz, and then a spectacular triumph at Berestesko in 1651 after the Tartars had defeated the insurgents. Earlier

Khmelnytsky, with much local anti-Polish support concluded an agreement with Tsar Alexis at Pereslavl which established his later credentials in history as the first Ukrainian friend of Russia and which enabled him to enter Kyiv. There, in alliance with the Khans of Crimea, Khmelnytsky set up an almost equally harsh regime. Hard pressed and losing followers he nevertheless proclaimed himself as "Prince of Russia" but neither the Poles nor Alexis had the energy to end his rule. In 1657 he died, a new Hetman of the Cossacks was a supporter of the Poles and Khmelnytsky's new son only a boy. A treaty with Poland was agreed in 1659 creating a "Duchy of Ruthenia" including Kyiv and the upper Dnieper but this arrangement was unacceptable to Tsar Alexis and George Khmelnytsky and hostilities opened in which Tartar and Ottoman armies also intervened to try and gain spoils. Eventually, in 1667 after much bloodshed and despite several Polish successes, by the Treaty of Andrusovo Ukraine was partitioned. Lands east of the Dnieper were to go to Russia, as was two years later Kyiv, the two years soon becoming permanent. Volhynia and Podolia were allowed to remain Polish. Worse was to follow, a weak Polish king bowing to a very powerful Ottoman invasion and in 1672 tamely surrendering what was left of Polish Ukraine to the Ottoman Sultan. The Cossack leader Doroszenko also submitted to Sultan Mahomet IV and Tartar rule was extended to Kharkiv and the Don River region.

The next Polish leader John Sobieski was very much more resolute and in a victorious campaign ejected the Ottomans, regained some of the lost territories and in the three subsequent years repelled three attempts by the Ottomans to return. Kamenets and parts of Podolia however still remained in Ottoman hands, one reason being the new menace of Russia where a Russian army had with great ferocity driven Tartars and Cossacks out of Kyiv. The Russians were unwilling to give any support to Sobieski and concluded a treaty with the Ottomans in 1681. Kyiv was now lost to the Poles forever. Believing that the Ottomans were the greatest danger to all Europe Sobieski, from 1674 King John III, in perhaps the greatest Polish moment in history led a multinational Christian army to defeat an Ottoman attempt to take Vienna in 1683. Success then left him. Tartar raids resumed, the lethargy that a hundred years later was to destroy Poland set in and an attempt to retake Moldova failed, the local peasant population opposed to any return of Polish rule in the Dniester area while the Russians seized the opportunity to reoccupy the northern Cherniyiv area of Ukraine in 1686. In the next year the Russians, their troops under the command of a Scots general, Patrick Gordon, opened a campaign against the Tartars in central Ukraine but were prevented from moving towards the Crimea when the Tartars set the grasslands on fire leaving no forage for the Russian cavalry. They were obliged to withdraw to a defensive line on the Dnieper.

In 1689, a year marking the end of a time of domestic turbulence, Moscow's new ruler, Peter I the Great was beginning to look for outlets to the seas, Black as well as Baltic. War against the Ottomans was declared in 1695. General Gordon reached Azov but it had been already seized by the Tartars and a Russian siege failed at their first attempt to take Azov (a defector had passed their plans to the Tartars, a move he was later under torture to regret). The next year it was taken by the Russians and an early example of Russian intervention outside their frontiers opened with Russian moves to protect the Christians in the Ottoman realms. In 1697 Gordon strengthened his hold on Taganrog and checked planned Tartar attacks on Ukrainian cities and towns.

The next conflict followed a new player on the scene, Sweden, whose ambitious soldier-king Charles XII sought to overrun Poland and with it north Ukraine. War with Russia began in 1705 Charles reducing the weak King of Poland (by origin the Elector of Saxony) to vassalage. After a short interlude in 1706 Charles was joined by Mazeppa, Hetman of the Cossacks and the Khan of the Crimea in a plan to attack Moscow from Ukraine, but first Mazeppa's followers and then Mazeppa himself defected. In a great battle at Poltava in north Ukraine Charles XII was decisively defeated, with Mazeppa fleeing to the Ottomans. This 1709 battle was a major step in the development of Russian domination of the Ukraine though further fighting was to follow before it was complete.

Charles XII fled to the Ottoman Empire; there he cobbled together a coalition of Ottomans and Poles. In a brief war in 1709-10 the Russians suffered a severe defeat and were obliged to surrender Azov, destroy their forts at Taganrog and to promise not to interfere in Poland. In the event Peter at first flatly refused to surrender Azov, but then Tartars swept across central Ukraine in a wave of destruction forcing Peter to agree to give up Azov. A formal agreement was reached in 1714 and the Russians agreed to make their administration in Ukraine where many preferred them to the Poles (who had deprived the Cossacks of the right to distil brandy, a measure much resented) more tolerant. But despite their success at Azov the Ottomans showed little interest in the area or in Ukraine. Russian interests were moving towards the Caucasus and the Urals and Peter and his successors did little to check the return of the long tradition of Tartar raids, these often extending to the Kyiv area. In one, Cyril Razumovski, a Hetman of the Cossacks with a claim to control territory on both banks of the Dnieper, proclaimed a Sovereign State of Ukraine in 1763. Russian authority was in some measure restored by the abolition of the Hetmanate in 1764 but a more effective reassertion required a more resolute policy from St Petersburg. This was to follow.

Chapter 3 Catherine the Great and "New Russia"

Earlier, in 1762 an event to foreshadow fundamental change in the region occurred with the accession to power of the Russian Empress Catherine II, a German princess married to the playboy dilettante Emperor Peter III whom she forced to abdicate and was to be murdered shortly afterwards. Under this formidable woman whose grand-scale private and public lives Russia was to make massive advances in many fields, only those concerned directly or indirectly with Ukraine can be noted here. In 1767 Ottoman Turkey declared war on Russia but at first made little effort to prosecute a campaign; in the next year in Kyiv a Cossack massacre of Roman Catholics, Jews and later Uniats began under the inspiration of two local leaders Gosta and Zhelezniak possibly but not certainly encouraged by Russia. In 1769 an Ottoman army some 200,000 strong and including Janissaries, Tartars and Ottomans attempted a full-scale invasion of Podolia but was decisively defeated by a Russian army very much smaller in size at a battle on the banks of the Kagul River. This victory, and others that followed in the Danube area led the Crimean Tartars to declare independence and the Ottomans to concede defeat with the signing of the Treaty of Kutchuk-Kainardji in 1774. By this treaty the Ottomans ceded the north Black Sea coast to Russia, recognised the independence of the Crimean Khans and Russians living in the Ottoman Empire were to be given toleration. A final clause set out the right of intervention if Orthodox Christians were molested, of especial interest as it was a second early assertion of a Russian right to intervene in another sovereign nation. A specific bonus for Ukraine was that a measure of Russian supervision ended the Crimean Khanate's practice of enslaving many hundreds of Slavs each year to be sent to the Istanbul slave markets.

A year before the Treaty Russia became heavily involved in containing and suppressing the massive 'Old Believers' two year long uprising in the Kuban area, led by Emilian Pugachev, a Don Cossack whose many followers include Upper Don Cossacks who had never accepted the Russian authority established by Peter the Great. The revolt lasted for two years but had the effect of temporarily stalling Russian ambitions. Very much more serious for peoples living in Ukraine, however, were the consequences of the decline and decay of Poland with its weak monarchy the subject of rivalries and the elective "one noble one vote" constitution simply providing a battleground for feuding factions. With three powerful neighbours, Habsburg Austria, Frederick the Great's Prussia and Catherine the Great's Russia all hungry for new territory Poland was subjected to the First Partition of 1772, central Ukraine going to Russia and Galicia, including Lviv to Austria, where it was to be renamed Lemberg. In St Petersburg Gregory Potemkin a man of relatively minor origins had made his way to power by his own skills, military prowess in several campaigns and in the bed of the Empress turned his attention to the Black Sea area where he had personal ambitions for some form of viceroyalty and Catherine sought a port on the Black Sea.

By 1777 no one was abiding by the 1774 treaty. The Crimean Khan had established a despotism, murdering his enemies, the Ottomans were reoccupying the Azov area and the Russians had attempted to settle Greeks in eastern Ukraine. Potemkin moved, entering the future new city of Kherson and the Crimean Khan's capital Bakhchisary in 1782, and with the aid of Suvorov the rising star of the Russian military formally annexing Crimea in the next year, local leaders all swearing loyalty to Catherine, the Ottomans conceding sovereignty in a treaty promising freedoms which were not fully honoured by the Imperial government. In the remaining fifteen years Russian rule was extended over all Ukraine together with the north Caucasus. Potemkin became the Governor-General, in Ukraine towns and villages were created, mocked as charades by some then and later but in practice to be future towns and cities. His energy was indefatigable. Land was given to Greeks and later Russian peasants, the Cossack Sech or strongholds destroyed. The first port to be developed was Kherson but ports and where necessary forts followed,

Sevastopol in 1783, Nikolayev in 1789 and intended to be a vice-regal capital, Ekaterinoslav (now Dniepropetrovsk) begun in 1787 after the ejection of the Zaporog Cossacks from the area. Their Hetman was despatched to the shores of the White Sea and Cossacks resettled in Astrakhan. In 1794 after Potemkin's death but on his orders the city of Odesa was founded. The city of Simferopol became the capital of the Crimea, where the Russians forced over half the Crimean Tartars into exile in Turkey, while encouraging Russians and a number of other European peoples to settle. Odesa grew very quickly as Russia's chief Black Sea port; its first local governor from 1803 to 1814 was a French aristocrat, the Duc de Richelieu in exile after the 1789 Revolution. The big Sech settlement of the Zaporog Cossacks had been destroyed on Catherine's orders and the Khanate of the Crimea stripped of all effective power. A Black Sea Fleet had been created. It is easy to mock Potemkin with his showy extravagance, at its height in 1787 when Catherine and Joseph II, the Emperor of Austria, visited Crimea, but his achievement should never be underestimated.

After the Third Partition in 1795 ended the existence of Poland the Russian empire's frontiers were to last until the end of the First World War, but the social order was common in areas acquired by Russia and Prussia with slightly better conditions in the Austrian area. In the Russian areas serfs had no civic rights until the Emancipation of Tsar Alexander II 1861. Grim poverty remained for men working on the large estates or smaller squires' domains. For many their interests became more class-bound resentment against landlord oppression than national, within their wretched lives religion providing the only comfort, even this, though, was to become increasingly linked and identified with the land-owning and later industrial establishment.

In Central and East Ukraine Catherine's "New Russia" had arrived.

Chapter 4 The Nineteenth Century and Pre 1914 Years

The destruction of the kingdom of Poland by the three successive late 18th Century partitions was to have major and lasting effects on the areas of Ukraine taken by Austria (later Austria-Hungary) and Russia, both afterwards and in horrific circumstances to be included within the territory of Ukraine.

Most of the area gained by Austria already had a considerable Polish population among communities of several other ethnicities including Jews and Ukrainians. The area around the city of Lviv in Galicia had a higher percentage of Galician peoples, more Ukrainian than Polish. But the Poles on land and in the towns were the property owners, exploiting labour on landed estates. The style of Austrian rule was generally moderate and tolerant, having earlier ruled the area the Poles saw no need for a new arrival assertion. In Vienna the Poles were seen as one of the three "ascendancy peoples" (the other two being the Austrians themselves and the Hungarians), whose responsibility it was to govern troublesome uncultured peoples such as the Bohemians and Moravians. Ukrainian nationalism was not seen as a danger, most Ukrainians in any case content not to be in Russia. The city of Lemberg became Polish with local power in the region resting with the nobility and squirearchy , in particular the Potocki family. Serfs in Poland had been freed briefly in 1794, and although serfdom was restored peasants retained rights over movement and produce. Their personal interests still lay more with their religious beliefs than a political opposition. The region's several different minorities, Hungarians, Jews, Greeks and others tended to settle in communities for social and security reasons but this was later to prove calamitous. The Austrian administration itself was one of an inefficient hidebound bureaucracy working in large, ugly and depressing buildings, but people could talk relatively freely so long as they did not go too far or take any direct political action. Lemberg received some very fine Western European style church and private buildings which are well preserved. The enormous area of the Habsburg dominions, comprising Galicia, south Poland, Hungary and Austria, until 1866 Venice, and later extending into Slovenia, Croatia and the Dalmatian Coast, was a free trade zone, providing great opportunities for trade, particularly after the construction of a railway system. The benefits extended to many petty entrepreneurs.

Life in the areas gained by Potemkin for Russia was very different. In 1863 addressing a devolved local Polish assembly largely composed of nobles and shortly after a nationalist uprising, Tsar Alexander II concluded with the words "Point des rêveries messieurs", 'Gentlemen let us have no dreams'. No dreams was to be the policy of post-occupation Russia and later Communist governments. Men of ability could develop their careers to very senior posts, local cultures could sing and dance, even speak in local languages, but must not entertain dreams of independence. The Russians felt, as a conquering newly arrived regime, a much greater need to impose an outward official conformism, assisted by the large-scale arrival of ethnic Russian immigrants, and in the latter part of the 19th Century secret police work. Nearly two million Ukrainians moved out of Ukraine to settle in Siberia and beyond. The benefits of economic union were mostly one way – to Russia. For day to day administration Russian Ukraine was divided into oblasti, regions in the same way as Russia proper.

Both Austrian and Russian Ukraine remained essentially large agricultural economies, not only wheat but also other products grown either by labour, serf until 1861 thereafter a rural proletariat, or poverty-stricken peasants living in wooden shacks. A measure of industry and railway construction began, for most of the century in central or western Ukraine – machinery and textiles to the prosperity of Odesa, food and shipbuilding at Mykolayiv (Nicolayev) and at the end of the century coal and metals in the east. These developments brought about two important social changes. In the east Russian men and families arrived to provide the work force in grim industrial towns. Odesa, which was a free port from 1815 to 1858, also attracted a Russian immigrant population together with smaller numbers of Greeks, Jews and many other peoples. The city acquired a cosmopolitan character, a cultural life at times Bohemian, and shady traders not always respectful of authority. The Crimea became heavily populated by Russians both as a warm weather holiday area and the base of the Black Sea Fleet.

In northern Ukraine a proto-nationalist 'Ukrainian consciousness' began to appear, Kyiv based, taking two forms. First was the widespread popularity of the poetry of Taras Shevchenko in which he wrote of the need for social justice, particularly for the peasantry, and an end to Tsarist rule. Related to his writings but also a product of Church influence were changes in the spoken word, differences between Ukrainian speakers and Russians. Shevchenko was exiled to Siberia for ten years, the conditions there leading to his premature death. In 1876 the Russian government banned all writing in Ukrainian, but followers of Shevchenko continued to write conveying the same messages; also the year 1876 saw peasants at a small town near Kyiv joining in a revolutionary plot, very quickly unearthed and suppressed.

In 1828 war broke out between Russia and the Ottoman Empire, fighting taking place on the Danube and Asia. The Zaporog Cossacks lent the Russians useful help, and for the Russians the war reinforced the value of her Black Sea Fleet. The Treaty of Adrianople in 1829 reiterated Russia's perception of a right to intervene if Christians in Turkey were persecuted.

War came to the Crimea in the conflict that carries the peninsula's name. Ostensibly the cause was the issue of protection of Christians in the Ottoman Empire, France claiming an especial role. In reality the issue at stake was the decline of the Ottoman Empire and the future of its remaining Danubian provinces. France, to be supported by Britain, feared a Russian dominance, perhaps even an occupation of Constantinople. Russian troops crossed the Pruth River in July 1853 but met with an initial setback. Royal Navy warships entered the Bosphorus in November and the Black Sea in

January 1854 after the Russian Navy had destroyed the Ottoman Navy at Sinope earlier in November. The French and British government entered the war on 28 March 1854. On 16 September British and French troops landed on the Crimean peninsula and began to advance on Sevastopol. There the military engineering genius Count Todleben began preparing a formidable defence system; the city's population, men, women and schoolchildren willingly providing labour. On 17 October the long siege began. In early 1855 Sardinia joined the British and French and a successful landing was made at Kerch. In the eleven months' siege there were six periods of artillery bombardments, the shortest two days, the longest six. A Russian attempt to break out from the city failed and eventually in September 1855 French troops stormed the forts and cities. The war's costs and casualties were bearing increasingly heavily on both sides and when in February Palmerston became Prime Minister and in March Tsar Nicholas died it seemed peace might be reached. There was however to be a final epic period of stiff fighting. Taganrog was bombarded from the sea, a Russian attempt to sortie out of besieged Sevastopol was blocked and the campaign only ended when on September 8 French troops stormed the last redoubt. Peace negotiations opened in February 1856 to be concluded in April, the Russians conceded the right for a Black Sea Fleet and the Ottomans promised tolerance for Christians. The Russians regained the right for a Black Sea Fleet in 1871 following an intervention by Bismarck, but in 1876 a new war between Russia and the Ottoman Empire opened – this time not directly involving Ukraine.

The main effects of the Crimean War on Ukrainians were twofold – enforced conscription of peasants and farm labourers, and the destruction of Sevastopol. The Russian army at the battle of Inkerman included four Ukrainian regiments, each of four battalions, Odesa, Dnieper, Ukraine and Azov, and a Cossack cavalry unit. The battalions will no doubt have included Russians and young men from other communities besides Ukrainians. The enormous Russian army, over 800,000 strong recruited by draft had neither the rifles nor the enterprise in action to counter the British and French assaults. At the end of the fighting the victors found Russian soldiers in flight deserting and the ruined city of Sevastopol acutely short of water, hospitals overcrowded and without drugs, worsened by outbreaks of cholera and typhus.

Periodic peasant and industrial worker rebellions and strikes, increasing numbers now literate broke out from time to time, one of the largest taking place in the streets of Kharkiv in 1886, but the only regime threatening crisis was that of 1905 opening, predictably, in Odesa with the 'Workers Revolution' of street riots and strikes in January that spread to other Russian cities including in Ukraine Kharkiv. In Odesa the cause of revolution was strengthened by the arrival of the battleship *Potemkin*, its crew in full mutiny. All uprisings were suppressed brutally, with bloodshed, but factory strikes, protesting against wretched pay and often dangerous conditions continued.

The century also saw periodic pogroms of the Jewish communities in Ukraine, the worst being in Odesa in 1905. In the Austrian region Ukrainian nationalist leaders were given varying prison sentences but none were shot. A Russian inspired irredentist movement appeared in 1908 but attracted little support. In September 1911 the reformist Prime Minister Stolypin was shot dead in the Kyiv Opera House. The motives of his assassin Bogrov are obscure; he was a Jewish lawyer, a socialist – and a police informer. His death ended the last chance of real reform in Tsarist Russia.

Chapter 5 The First World War and its Aftermath

In the rival Russian and Austrian armies that mobilised for the outbreak of war in July and August 1914 were large numbers of men who at the time were living in the Russian or Austrian region of Ukraine. Ukrainian accounts suggest over 3 million served in the Russian army and a quarter of a million in the Austrian. These figures must be viewed with caution, a very large number of their kinsmen and if they survived descendants will not now be living in Ukraine, following the violent events of the next eight years. Accurate figures are impossible to ascertain.

The military campaigns swung from one side to the other, often dependent on priority calls on either army for reinforcements elsewhere. The Austrian army entering Galicia on 10 August gained an apparent initial success but were checked and reversed by the Russians, who inflicted a catastrophic defeat on the Austrians, occupying Lemberg and most of Galicia. In March 1915 this situation was also reversed when the Austrians in cooperation with the Germans recovered Galicia even entering into Russian Ukraine. This success was also to be reversed in the summer of 1916 when the very able Russian General Brusilov ejected the Austrians in the last campaign of the army of a Russian Tsar. In 1915 and 1916 the Austrians raised a Ukrainian Legion to fight for them against the Russians, the Legion was to figure in the events to follow, as was the anarchistic Cossack "Black Army" of Nestor Makhno engaged in guerrilla warfare in central Ukraine.

The November 1917 revolution in St Petersburg and the fall of the Monarchy let loose a wide variety of revolutionary groups and activists across the former Russian empire. Among the policies, and to be immediate priorities, for Sovnarkom, the Council of People's Commissars, were decrees to smash all groups not following its Leninist revolutionary ideology, banning of publications arguing other views, and a decree that all the regions of the former empire were now under its authority, all attempts at secession by any region or group were to be banned – in essence the Soviet view until 1991 and arguably since. At the time though the Communists were weak on the international stage and were obliged to allow German troops to enter the north of Ukraine and in August 1918 to land on the Crimean peninsula and Odesa, the aim being the possibility of using Russian warships in an operation combined with the Austrian navy to defeat the Allied navies in the eastern Mediterranean. The Germans had unwisely believed that a Kyiv Cossack leader, Hetman Skoropadsky would be able to head an independent pro-German regime and signed an agreement with him to that effect and to provide urgently needed grain to counter the Royal Navy blockade of Germany. Skoropadsky had no following and was forced to flee for his life. After the November 1918 Armistice the German forces were withdrawn. French forces then arrived in Odesa ending a short-lived Odesa People's Republic. These and British military support for anti-Bolshevik forces in eastern Ukraine were withdrawn later in 1919.

As chaos worsened, different factions appeared in Russian Ukraine. Demonstrations by street workers and peasants in Ukraine led to the formation of a Leninist "Ukrainian Soviet Socialist Republic" being proclaimed in Kyiv, only to be opposed by the "Black Army" and other factions assisted where possible. In the Austrian Galicia region a pro-Russian West Ukrainian Republic was proclaimed, but the most effective new leader was a Cossack Hetman, Semyon Petlura, who sought a Ukraine neither Russian nor Polish but truly independent. Outside Ukraine, but with strong anti-Russian views was the new Polish leader Josef Pilsudski with a vision in general of a Polish Ukrainian alliance to contain the spread of Leninism and in particular of regaining the areas taken from Poland in 1772. His vision was not acceptable to Petlura, now Prime Minister in a unifying national government. At Versailles the peace-makers realising that without considerable further military expenditure there was little that they could do in eastern Europe and Ukraine other than propose a Polish administration in eastern Galicia to last for twenty-five years and be followed by a plebiscite, a proposal totally ignored.

Pilsudski's hurriedly formed and assembled Polish army held off a Ukrainian nationalist force that were trying to assert control in Galicia, even occupying half of Lviv but fighting in eastern Galicia continued in 1918 and 1919. In early 1920 Pilsudski reached an agreement with Petlura that Poland might retain the Lviv area in return for aid in liberating the rest of Ukraine from the Bolsheviks. In April the Polish advance began. Polish troops entered Zhitomir on 26 April and Kyiv on 8 May capturing a large number of Bolshevik soldiers. However, by June the Bolsheviks now freed from major civil war commitments and under the command of the able but very ruthless generals Tukhachevsky and Budenny forced the Poles into full retreat.

The government of Lenin then ordered a full advance on Warsaw to reconquer pre-1914 Poland and destabilise Germany. Bypassing Lviv Tukhachevsky advanced on the Polish capital but was checked and defeated by Pilsudski at the battle of Warsaw in August 1920, a battle foreshadowing the nature of the Second World War and the 1945-1991 "Cold War", wider issues of ideology and race replacing narrower disputes over territory. By the Treaty of Riga, agreed in March 1921 Poland renounced any general claim for rule in Ukraine but retained Eastern Galicia. Lviv returned to the former Polish name Lwow for an eighteen-year ceasefire. Petlura, in exile in Paris, was assassinated by Soviet agents in 1926.

The "White Russian" military operations against the Bolsheviks, to last from 1918 to 1920 and supported with decreasing enthusiasm by Britain and France, imposed severe suffering in many areas of Russia, in the case of Ukraine the eastern Don area and Crimea. Villages were burnt, women raped and men, including priests, tortured. Some rural communities revolted against the Bolshevik requisitions only to bring further suffering. The 1920 final evacuations of the British and French military personnel besieged by terrified

Russian women and men for a place on the deck of a ship ended six years of warfare in which an estimated total of over one and a half million people had died. Unfortunately for Ukraine worse, in the form of Red Terror was to follow.

Chapter 6 Communist Ukraine 1920-1941

The fighting and civil war strife of the previous seven years left the 1920 Soviet leadership with a chaotic situation in Russia, in particular Ukraine. Many landlords had been murdered or driven from productive estates; the new occupiers were smallholders not capable of producing the same quantities of grain or other foods. Factories were smashed, and the railways in need of long periods for repair. Peoples had moved, often into slum suburbs composed of shacks, town populations had increased including numbers of women. Particularly in towns men from different communities had become mixed which together with the limited education many had managed to gain had served to forge a bitter class-based unity. Fired by propaganda and rhetoric the Bolsheviks had been able to launch an elimination of the former imperial middle and official classes, often by a death after agonising, long-duration torture, throughout 1919 and 1920. Victims were not limited to land and factory owners but also extended to any who showed some humane consideration towards them, a class war in which prisoners were taken only for sadistic pleasure. The political infighting in Russia between Lenin, Trotsky and Stalin in which after the death of Lenin in 1924 Stalin was to emerge all-powerful lies outside the scope of this work, but all saw the Terror campaign of the Red Army and Cheka political police as essential, in no way to be mitigated or regretted.

For Ukraine the immediate consequence of this First Red Terror was famine, many hundreds dying if not directly of starvation but of malnutrition and its consequences.

At the height of the failure the regime created an institution of the greatest importance, the State Planning Commission, Gosplan which in 1924 produced a national strategy, the First Five Year Plan (in the event declared completed after four and a half years). The two foundations of the plan, for all the Soviet Union, were industrialisation and collectivisation. The whole philosophy of Marxism was seen to be based on an industrial proletariat which in pre-Revolution Russia was relatively small; but a Marxist state could not be built on peasant producers. For reasons then both political and national a massive industrial development programme was the top priority. Major industrial schemes in particular electric and hydro-electric, chemical, motor car, aircraft and transport projects were all set in hand in feverish haste, for Ukraine the show piece being the huge Dnepropetrovsk hydro-electric power plant. While others were generally situated in the Urals or Siberia beyond the range of attacks by an enemy, the industrial foundations already laid in eastern Ukraine were developed, the arriving workforce to total one and a half million by 1939 being mainly Russian saw themselves as liberated from serfdom and with a prospect of an improved standard of living in the new town. Workers who exceeded norms of hours or production were publicised as heroes, most notably later in 1935 the Donets miner Stakhanov, his name becoming a movement. For the workers blocks of flats composed of small rooms and shared ablutions were built. Trade unions no longer functioned as such, being transformed into agents of the state. The programme was continued with the Second Development Programme of 1933 to 1937; by the outbreak of war in 1939 the Soviet Union was becoming one of the world's major industrial nations with in respect of military equipment a lead in tank design, a by-product of the vital Machine Tractor Stations programme. But not all products were of durable quality, a consequence of the haste.

Collectivisation was more difficult and controversial, but peasant smallholding was already showing itself unable to meet food requirements; equally important individual smallholder proprietors could have no place in the new post-Revolution Marxist state. Targeting of peasants, especially any believed to be working for their own profit began from 1922 onwards but only became systematic and wholesale from 1925 onwards when the second Red Terror was launched. Troops, police, party activists descended on the terrified smallholders forcing them into the new collective farms 'kolkhozes'. Initially these were designed to reduce the individual to being a unit of labour, all the produce of the land allocated to a particular collective was to be at the disposal of the state; in return local level institutions on the farm or in a group of farms would provide a small wage payment, food, later a small private garden, a literacy campaign and basic medical service. Opposition to being dragooned into collectives was stiff, especially in north Ukraine; from 1925 to 1928 rural Russia became pandemonium. Peasants were described as rich and exploitative "Kulaks", the last survivors of landlordism to be eliminated. Thousands were packed off to Siberia or to labour camps, others escaping the forced marches to a collective, moved to the cities to find paid work, others to the new Arctic Circle penal labour camps, later called Gulags. The result inevitably was famine conditions, made worse by drought and bad weather and especially severe in north Ukraine, an area from Petlura days especially distrusted by Stalin. The whole process was concealed from the world by a torrential rhetoric describing collectivisation as the destruction of bloodsuckers and bourgeois remnants. The various agents of the Terror were devoid of any humanity, themselves the victims of calculated psychological brainwashing.

The Third Terror, Stalin's notorious purges took place between 1936 and 1938 and was largely directed against Bolshevik leaders at the time of the Revolution and the early 1920s, a swathe of lower level Party members and officials, professional men including doctors, engineers, writers, scientists and teachers and several hundred of the ablest military. Tried in secret conclaves before a 'court' composed of members who knew if they failed to convict that they would be the next victims; the accused were denounced as conspirators against the regime in alliances with France, Britain, exiled refugees, former monarchists. Scores of thousands throughout the Soviet Union including Ukraine were shot, imprisoned or sent to labour camps. Defenders of the Soviet regime have claimed that the real aim of this Terror was the establishment of the total autocracy of Stalin, and necessary for the preparations for a great war in which Stalin was to be the victor. Others argue that the poor performance of the Red Army in the 1939-40 Winter War in Finland and its incompetent performance in 1941, especially in the major defeats in Ukraine, must be laid at Stalin's door and could have been averted had he been prepared to listen to wiser advice.

Within the Constitutions of the Soviet Union, those of 1922 and 1936 Ukraine was given paper autonomy as the Ukraine Socialist Soviet Republic, but within this Crimea was retained in the Russian Socialist Federal Republic. The capital of Ukraine was returned to Kyiv from Kharkiv in 1934. By 1939 the standard of living in towns and on the land had improved a little, if not greatly from the standards of 1914. Many were impressed by the development of industry and still subscribing to revolutionary enthusiasm and pride. But for thousands of others life remained a dark awareness of fear, the knock on the door, the basis of 1920s and 1930s Communist rule throughout the Soviet Union.

Chapter 7 The Second World War 1941-1945

The Second World War was an even more horrific experience for the people of Ukraine than the 1930s. Following the Ribbentrop-Molotov August 1939 agreement, the Red Army entered Poland on 17 September 1939 and occupied most of western Ukraine including the city and region of Lviv. These areas were then joined onto the Soviet Republic of Ukraine, the Polish property owners were expropriated and Communist programmes initiated.

In central Ukraine the extreme Right wing elements within Ukrainian nationalism mindful of the Soviet brutalities in Ukraine in the 1930s saw the changing situation as one of possible opportunities, anticipating correctly that a German-Soviet conflict was inevitable. Secret contacts had been made even before the start of the German invasion opening on 22 June 1941. The Germans accordingly played down their racial contempt for 'sklavische Untermenschen' (Slav sub-humans) at this stage, seeing that in an occupied Ukraine, Right Wing nationalists could be useful in the necessary controlling of other communities, Poles and Russians. When the campaign opened the Red Army was severely handicapped by poor generals appointed for political reasons and the setting aside by Stalin of the clear warnings of German plans given to him by his own military staff and by Great Britain. The Red Army suffered heavy defeats especially in Ukraine where 600,000 men, many Ukrainian, were surrounded and taken prisoner. So, for many nationalists it appeared that their day had come. With German support a racially purified Ukrainian state could emerge under German protection, freed at last from Russian, Tsarist or Soviet domination. Nazism and its methods were seen as justifiable, indeed admired by many, in particular among the local gendarmerie. German Army regiments to their surprise often received a warm welcome on their arrival, soon occupying Odesa, and entering Kyiv in August 1941. The retreating Soviets had mined city buildings causing them casualties and a first round of destruction. The occupation of

Ukraine was followed immediately by a large-scale, carefully organised campaign to exterminate Jews in Ukraine. Between 29 and 30 September huge mass slaughter took place at Babyn Yar, Berdichev, Kamenets Podolsk, Lviv and southern Volhynia. Different totals of the numbers massacred, some figures including later victims have appeared, the most reliable suggest at least a million if not more died in this period. Some were subjected to torture first, others simply rounded up and placed before firing squads. At Babyn Yar where figures are reliable 34,000 Kyiv Jews died in three days of massacre. Elsewhere Jewish villages and settlements were burnt to the ground.

Resistance by peoples of Ukraine was, predictably, polarised. The Soviet government began organising partisan resistance in occupied Russia and Ukraine as early as the summer of 1941. Operating in forests partisans controlled by the Soviet command attacked railway lines and road supply transport. Much extolled by propaganda their impact was limited, perhaps intelligence gathering being the greatest use. The numbers of partisans grew in 1943, some 20,000 being active in Ukraine in mid-1943 to peak to half a million by the last year of the occupation, about 50% being Ukrainian. But they were not always able to count on covert public support, memories of the Red Terrors still burning in the north of Ukraine.

Also fired by memories of the 1930s as well as nationalism was the Organisation of Ukrainian Nationalists, OUN, who admired Nazi ideas of a racially pure nation. The OUN sponsored a Ukrainian Peoples Army, UPA, whose activities reflected OUN views, especially in western Ukraine in 1943 attacking and killing Poles and Jews. There among the Poles the UPA came to serve as a recruiting agent for the Soviet sponsored Polish and several Ukrainian partisan brigades; in turn this led some Ukrainian fighters to cooperate with the Germans in their historic hatred of the Poles. The UPA's most striking achievement, clearly indicating its Ukraine for the Ukrainians and no one else racism was the assassination of one of the ablest of the Soviet generals, Vatutin, who had just driven the Germans out of Kyiv in 1944.

Another anti-Soviet organisation to include large numbers of Ukrainians was the Russian Liberation Army founded by a one-time distinguished Soviet General, Vlasov, who had been captured by the Germans and had become disillusioned with the Soviet Union of Stalin. His force, recruited from Germans, held over 90,000 prisoners at its peak. The Vlasov units were not employed against the Red Army, but used against partisans in Czechoslovakia or in less politically dangerous operations such as the guarding of prisoners of war camps, or military administration and labour duties in cities that had suffered heavy British air attacks such as Dresden in February 1945. In the last months of the war there were numerous desertions some even trying to rejoin the Red Army. After the end of the war and recapture by the Soviets executions, often after torture, followed.

Odesa being available as a naval base after its capture by the German army, troops landed at Kerch and fought their way across the Crimean peninsula to open, in October 1941, a three hundred day siege of Sevastopol. Local Ukrainian partisans played a gallant role in the fighting in the city's catacombs. At the end of the siege in June 1942 the city was devastated, its buildings destroyed and hundreds of citizens killed, the survivors starving and any identified as having collaborated with the Germans meeting an unpleasant end. By the autumn of 1942 it was becoming clear that the Germans were in difficulties, neither of the two key cities, Moscow and Leningrad, had been taken and their spectacular advance across Ukraine, despite the capture of the major cities, eventually including Kharkiv, turned to retreat in early 1943. German policy for the retreat was "scorched earth" total destruction of anything that could be of use to the advancing Red Army. In Ukraine itself the local real intentions of the Nazi policy, a colonialist occupation of Ukraine by German settler farmers had become clear, dispelling all illusions. By late 1944 the German Army had been cleared out of Ukraine and scores against those who had earlier collaborated with the Reichskommissariat were being settled. By the end of the year most of the gendarmes had deserted the Germans, a number signing up with the Ukraine Partisan Army to finish off the remaining Jews and Poles, the curtain raiser for new civil wars and ethic cleansing to last well into 1946 and 1947. The partisan leader Stepan Bandera was portrayed to some effect as a Fascist by Moscow.

For ordinary Ukrainian people, peasants, workers, city dwellers, the war was a struggle for any food, shelter or warmth available. Many elderly men, women and children were drafted into forced labour by whichever army was in their area, at least 15,000 were employed building a huge headquarters for Hitler near Vinnitsa in 1942-43. One community to suffer especially severely were the Tartars of Crimea whom Stalin suspected of disloyalty. Some 180,000, together with a number of other Ukrainians also suspect were packed off to Siberia in crowded goods wagons in May 1944, causing great suffering and hardship.

Two million Ukrainians had been drafted and served in the Red Army in the fierce and harsh conditions of the Eastern Front, estimates of a million and a quarter being killed or dying. The lowest estimate of civilian deaths is six million including the Jewish massacres. Survivors returned to find their homes and livelihood destroyed, in rural areas several quite often finding themselves as the sole or perhaps one of two or three male survivors of their pre-1941 community. In cities such as Kyiv over 80 per cent of the buildings were destroyed.

The sufferings of the peoples of Ukraine in the Second World War can only be exceeded by that of the Jews in horror and misery. The scars left by the events of 1941-47 were to last, although very different perceptions of them have been argued subsequently.

Chapter 8 The Soviet Union 1945-1991

For many the German surrender in May 1945 brought no relief from fighting, suffering and genocide as civil wars spread over western Ukraine. The Poles sought to retain their position, villages and communities. Ukrainians, Russians and others sought to exterminate them. The violence of the fighting, little reported in Western Europe must rate among the very worst example of man's inhumanity to man, wholesale massacres with especial forms of lingering physical suffering on men, women and children and the destruction amounting to the careful and deliberate erasing of all traces of former villages and settlements throughout western Ukraine and Volhynia. The Poles in turn defended themselves as best they could, imploring Soviet help not often forthcoming. Figures of the deaths vary greatly according to the nationality of the providers but a minimum estimate may be made: by the end of 1946 some 90,000 Poles and 20,000 Ukrainians had died. The Soviet government decided that the only solution to these mass killings was the delineation of frontiers and the forcible resettlement of ethnicities within them, moves of whole populations irrespective of the amount of suffering it would cause. Mass deportations then began wholesale, by trainload or if the distances were not too great on foot, men, women and children obliged to leave all property behind. These draconian measures at least lowered the kill rate. To try and regain some Ukrainian support the city of Lviv (Lemberg again under the Germans) and its region were brought back to Ukraine with the Ukrainian name Lviv. Resettlement by Russians and some east Ukrainians followed.

The new Communist government and army of Poland in reprisal turned to ejection, "repatriation", of Ukrainian communities in south-east Poland, some 40,000 being expelled after numerous village massacres. In March 1947 the Polish Minister for Defence was assassinated by a Ukrainian UPA group, an incident leading to Operation *Vistula*. In the course of this the remaining Ukrainians in Poland were taken on long cattle-truck rail journeys to the regions of former northeast Germany and East Prussia for "resettlement", usually in localities where the best land plots had already been taken. There they were subjected to an enforced culture rebranding – only Polish spoken in schools and business, Ukrainian forbidden, Roman Catholic only worship, Polish and not Ukrainian dress, music, dance and celebration. Spasmodic UPA guerrilla attacks in south west Ukraine continued until the early 1950s and a shadow government in exile under Bandera existed briefly. Bandera himself was murdered by the KGB in 1959 while in exile in Germany.

Stalin carried his frontiers ideas still further forward with his views that the eastern European countries liberated by the Red Army must have pro-Soviet governments even if they did not want them, and that these governments would obediently follow Moscow's policies in the now developing Cold War. The frontiers of eastern Europe were accordingly drawn to ensure Moscow control, at least a strip of land if not more linking Romania, Hungary, Czechoslovakia and Poland either with the Russian state or one of the Soviet Union border republics. This arrangement enabled the Soviet Army (as the Red Army was now renamed) to launch incursions into Hungary in 1956 and Czechoslovakia in 1968, both from Ukraine. In both cases the tank divisions must have contained a large number of Ukrainian conscripts.

Also on the international stage Stalin secured full United Nations membership for two of the border republics, Belarus and Ukraine. His claim for this was Great Britain's insistence on membership for Canada, Australia, New Zealand and South Africa. Ukraine's membership did provide a measure of local satisfaction and pride, but neither of the two border republics ever voted differently from the line taken by the Kremlin.

Within the Soviet Union itself the last seven years of Stalin's rule were masked by a fresh political purge, further massive industrialisation and hagiographic personal propaganda. The industrialisation had by 1955 doubled Ukraine's production with massive further development of mining and industrial manufacture, much but by no means all in the eastern regions of Ukraine. New fields included computer technology and aircraft manufacture. The post-war rebuilding of shattered cities and towns was also an urgent priority. The political purge was directed generally against any who opposed the now totally authoritarian rule of Stalin for whom age had transformed an already highly suspicious nature into paranoia. All officials, party activists and cultural figures were brought firmly to heel while the particular targets, military leaders, the Leningrad party and official administration and the remaining Jewish community were very harshly victimised. In one respect this last of Stalin's purges was one small degree more moderate, the old atmosphere of dread returned and the early morning knock on the door continued, but the secret police (N.K.V.D., later the K.G.B.) preferred exile to labour camps in the Gulag archipelago and elsewhere to execution. Blaring propaganda presented Stalin as omniscient; all meetings were required to praise him. Also developed were Cold War themes and the necessity for ideological purity, in this context hero-worship of Stalin carried to extreme degrees. The constitution of the Soviet Union was updated to include its new Baltic states and other members, but the 'let us have no dreams' message remained. The border republics were firmly reminded that patriotism was for the Soviet Union, nationalism must remain cultural only. No non-Slav men were appointed to the Politburo, Russian minorities were built up in the border republics and their economies developed to be dependent either upon Russian factory processing of raw materials or Russian markets for the sale of locally produced goods.

Stalin died in 1953, his successors being left with his legacy, for which open apologies were soon necessary, notably the speech by Nikita Khrushchev in revealing the full details of Stalin's 'personality cult'. Life otherwise became tolerable for Soviet citizens, the early morning knock on the door soon ended and peoples, including those in Ukraine given what they really wanted, peace and economic stability even if it meant queues. Housing, in the form of huge and ugly blocks of flats improved. Schools, technical institutes and universities were developed, dispensaries and hospitals founded. General politics, and freedom of expression or travel, had never been a major desire of people, the measures granted locally, representation and debate over local issues, sufficed. Order mattered more than the corruption, favouritism and nepotism to become increasingly obvious in the 1970s and 1980s within the Soviet system. Daily queues for basic needs while the favoured enjoyed special perquisites, and brutal military service for conscripts were all accepted as part of life. Many peoples, especially in Ukraine either from their own memories of from accounts provided by their sons and daughters, view the 1960s and 1970s as a 'golden age'.

Of Stalin's successors Khrushchev, a Ukrainian who after a transition period achieved the leadership in 1958, was the most important. While continuing the Cold War – and accepting a major political defeat during the 1962 Cuba Missile Crisis, Khrushchev was seen to be the bringer of change and development. He also, unusually among Russian and Soviet leaders, had a sense of humour which resonated giving him a personal humanity. For Ukraine he arranged the transfer of the Crimean Peninsula from the Russian to the Ukrainian Republic. The transfer was not seen as of any great significance at the time, no one believed that the Soviet Union might disintegrate. The exiled Crimean Tartars began to return to the peninsula in the late 1980s, but were not restored to their land holdings. Many tried to settle on unused land and violent clashes broke out, to last for several months.

One disaster to befall Ukraine in April 1986 was the major steam and nuclear explosion at the Chernobyl power plant when over eight tons of radioactive fallout was blown north and west, over west Ukraine and Belarus. Thirty-one people were killed or died shortly after, and 135,000 people had to be evacuated, many permanently. Published casualty figures suggest some 4,000 died later as a consequence of disease caused by the explosion with over 160,000 including

2,000 children suffered life-threatening disease consequences. The Soviet government at first concealed news of the disaster for two days and later continually tried to play down the consequences.

Khrushchev was gently removed from power by his colleagues in 1964. He was blamed for the failures of his diplomacy in the Cuban Missile crisis and in grand scale agricultural development projects.) The next three leaders all appeared to think that attaining power was an end in itself after which little more remained to be done. The first of these was a Ukrainian, Leonid Brezhnev, in power from 1964 to 1982, then Yuri Andropov from 1982 to 1984, a hard-liner who tried to discipline the regime but was terminally ill, and Constantine Chernenko from 1984 to 1985, a man of very limited ability and personal illness. All in practice permitted the system to drift. For the individual in the street, now after a period of stability more street-wise, the vast network of corruption, shady marketing, favouritism, nepotism, special privileges for the party elite were by this time only too obvious. For the whole nation, the inability to develop the standard of living of citizens, now increasingly interested in consumer goods, the inability of Soviet industry to match that of the United States and above all the huge costs of the Soviet Union's military forces in their efforts to equal the power of the United States (particularly the crushing costs of the last class of inter-continental ballistic missile submarines) were a triple burden that the regime could not sustain. Protest demonstrations first appeared in Lviv in 1988 with marches and hunger strikes in Kyiv in 1990. Protest movements demanding independence emerged, notably the Uniat Church released from Stalin's 1946 ban and a Ukrainian People's Movement for Restructuring, Rukh.

The last Soviet leader, Mikhail Gorbachev who came to power in 1985 attempted reforms to include social bridge-building and greater freedom to speak and call the system to account, only met the failure of all who try to reform authoritarian regimes – once criticism is permitted it cannot be controlled. Unrest broke out in Georgia, Latvia and Lithuania, all suppressed sharply by the police. While out of Moscow a coup in August 1991 overthrew Gorbachev and shortly afterwards in December 1991 the Soviet Union ceased to exist. The border Republics suddenly became fully independent nations. Russia's new alcohol addicted ruler Boris Yeltsin had, predictably from a Soviet upbringing, no idea whatever on how to manage a free economy with disastrous private sell off results and increased costs for the man in the street. Now generally derided for his total incompetence Yeltsin nevertheless deserves real credit for certain achievements conveniently overlooked: the most free press in Russian history, freedom of teaching, research, access to archives and a genuine desire to be part of European life and culture.

A pedestrian strolling down the Nevski Prospekt in St Petersburg will see two cathedrals. On one side of the road is the Cathedral of the Spilled Blood, built to mark the site of Tsar Alexander II's assassination, a building of multiple onion shaped domes and mosaic walls, traditional Russian in style. On the other side he will see the Kazan Cathedral, built in 1810-1811 modelled on St Peter's in Rome with colonnades and a single cupola dome. The contrast summarises the dualism throughout Russian history, which identity to pursue – the authoritarian path of the Tsars and Stalin, or the more western path of Kerensky and Yeltsin. Unfortunately for its neighbours near and far the authoritarian path has been preferred for most of the nation's past.

Chapter 9 Independent Ukraine 1991-2014

On 24 August 1991 the Speaker of the Ukraine Supreme Council, Verkhovna Rada, Stanyslav Hurenko in somewhat earthy language urged the Council to vote immediately for independence. A referendum held in December produced an 84% Yes vote and Leonid Kravchuk was elected President of the new nation with a population of at least 52 million. Of this total some 75% were, and still are, ethnically Ukrainian though many were Russian speakers, 17% ethnically Russian living mostly in Crimea, Odesa and the east, 250,000 were Crimean Tartars and smaller numbers of Poles, Jews, Moldavians and Romanians. The nation's industry was entirely integrated into Russian plans and projects but in 1990-1991 was already in difficulties. The country's official language was declared to be Ukrainian with the exception of the Crimean Peninsula where Russian was given equal status.

The existing recession worsened, G.D.P. fell, inflation spiralled. Industrial unrest and, worse than strikes, massive corruption spread over the whole country. As a consequence the Kravchuk government fell in September 1992 and was replaced by Leonid Kuchma, a Russian language speaker who found difficulty in speaking in Ukrainian and whose policies were generally pro-Russian. Kuchma reformed the Republic's constitution to provide much greater executive powers, especially in defence, internal security and foreign affairs during his five-year term. The 450 strong parliament retained power to nominate or approve the prime minister and cabinet. Kuchma used his new powers to favour his friends and supporters when privatising state companies with cronyism in most fields. An outspoken journalist critical of Kuchma, Gongadze, met an unpleasant death in 2000; reports and rumours claimed that Kuchma was complicit. Although the economy stabilised and began to develop corruption still flourished and the reformist pro-European and NATO prime minister Viktor Yushenko was obliged to stand down.

The result was the 'Orange Revolution' of late 2004. Kuchma sought as his successor another strong pro-Russian, Viktor Yanukovich, who drew strong support from eastern Ukraine but was challenged by Yushenko over a two-month very bitter election campaign. In the course of this Yushenko's physical appearance changed, the result of dioxin poisoning. The first 31 October election result was not conclusive and another more decisive took place on 21 November, Yanukovich the apparent winner. Foreign election observers reported that this election had very clearly been rigged. Huge orange banner-waving crowds then took to the streets, despite the freezing temperatures, surrounding the parliament building and setting up camps for protestors in the Krushchatyk main street highway of Kyiv. The crowds were addressed, to wild applause by Yushenko and his attractive ally Yulia Tymoshenko. The Supreme Court annulled the earlier election and following a further campaign in which Yushenko was able to draw on Western funding and political advice. He became President in January 2005 with the well-coiffured Tymoshenko as prime minister and Yanukovich in opposition.

Yushenko's rule was however short-lived. He was himself weak, he and Tymoshenko fell out, as he was to do with many other supporters. Culture with an anti-Russian tone was encouraged and history books rewritten to castigate "the occupier". Ukrainian, now some 10% different from Russian, was made the sole official language. To mark Moscow's disapproval Russia then cut off oil supplies on 1 January, demanding an over four-fold increase in price. A snap election took place in September 2007, returning Tymoshenko as prime minister, but another financial crisis hit the Ukraine economy in 2008-9, worsened by a second suspension of Russian gas supplies in 2009. Moscow's pressure brought results in elections in 2010 when Yanukovich was re-elected with a little less than 50% of the votes cast. Yanukovich then returned to policies of closer ties with Russia and distancing himself and his supporters from closer ties with the European Union. The Russian language was now permitted in courts and official business. Yanukovich's prime minister Mykola Azarov observed, "Everything depends on the goodwill of the Russians, we are like Serfs". Yulia Tymoshenko was arrested and imprisoned in conditions that worsened her already existing medical problems. The gas problem was eased by Russia waiving a proportion of payments in return for an extension of the lease of Sevastopol, but overall trade and production fell. Corruption in its enormous scale was now led by the President's personal plans for his palace and the behaviour of his son. Officials' salaries were kept low, their masters knowing that their juniors would recoup by bribery.

In the bitter atmosphere created by this succession of events political faction and propaganda fighting broke out in late 2013 and early 2014. Ukrainian nationalist groups, the Stepan Bandera Trident and later the Right Sector roamed the streets of Odesa and elsewhere, people were killed. On 21 February 2014 Yanukovich and opposition leaders agreed to return to the 2004 Constitution (an agreement facilitated by the European Union), the release from prison of Tymoshenko whose sufferings were attracting widespread international criticism, and elections as soon as possible.

The next day, amid violent and noisy protests from protesters who had been camping out in Kiev's main Independence Square the Ukrainian Parliament dismissed Yanukovich who it transpired later had fled to Russia. A Kyiv street coup administration, claiming legality over the entire nation was formed with Oleksandr Turchynov as interim

President and Arseniy Yatsenyuk as prime minister. They were not recognised by the pro-Russian officials and political leaders in the east of the country. A whole new series of events were to follow, involving foreign countries nearby and further afield where Ukraine had not figured significantly in international or military issues.

At independence Ukraine was technically a nuclear power, parts of the Soviet Union's vast armoury of nuclear weaponry being stationed in Ukraine with many Ukrainian draft personnel in these and other units. Ukraine was willing to join Yeltsin's Commonwealth of Associated States which included all the former Soviet Union border republics except the three Baltic nations which all refused to join. Ukraine, however, refused to join Yeltsin's joint general-purpose military force and began a two-year period of defence re-structuring. By 1994 the country was non-nuclear (though Russian naval forces based on Sevastopol will no doubt have kept their nuclear weaponry). The Army which had a paper strength independence of some 220,000 was reduced to 187,000 by 1997 and 70,000 by 2011, the Navy from 16,000 to 11,000 and the Air Force from 150,000 to 45,000. For Sevastopol, Russia's only Black Sea naval base of any importance there was an initial two-year transition period in which authority was shared, this was followed in 1997 by a short-term ten-year lease agreement for the base which Yanukovich later extended for a further twenty-five years, to the fury of the Ukrainian nationalist opposition and the joy of the city's 70 per cent Russian population. Russian navy personnel in 1991 were given a two-year period to decide whether to serve in the Russian or Ukrainian navies. Most decided on the basis of their ethnicity but for some other issues – family or marriage connections, career prospects, pensions, affected choice. No one ever envisaged any confrontation or hostility between the two nations, and the Ukrainian Navy moved out to Odesa.

A unit of the Ukrainian Army was sent to join the United Nations operating in Bosnia-Herzegovina in the 1990s. It did not distinguish itself, being poorly trained and led, with both poor soldier motivation and a tendency for soldiers to market their stores, especially motor vehicle fuel to local people.

This indiscipline was just one example of the moral state of Ukraine in February 2014. The centuries of rule by the Tsars and then by the Communists had left a moral emptiness. Christian teachings applied to family life but since the state ignored them they were not relevant. Ethnic issues it appeared could in the end only be settled by violence. For the ordinary street dweller, ethnic Ukrainian or Russian, life had been a defence against authority, oppressive and corrupt officials, and police forces with no real concern for ordinary citizens. Any seizures of goods at the expense of authority were often simply plain common sense, necessary for the survival of families, the wage earner receiving totally inadequate pay. The majority of the population, now 10 per cent smaller than at independence following emigration abroad, had desired little more than calm and stability with perhaps a *toska*, a depressed nostalgic longing for a return to Russia among Russian speakers in Crimea and the east. But the majority of Russian speakers elsewhere would be content with a measure of devolution for most of the Russian areas, respecting their local culture and language but far from wishing for a return to Russia itself.

By early 2014 though, the tsunami of extreme ethnic and ideological rhetoric voiced by faction leaders had come to reawaken historic passions, distort reason and dehumanise even ordinary individuals. Faction leaders presented their opponents as sub-human, the pro-Russian activists and provocateurs denounced the nationalists as the Banderovtsi, 1941-45 type fascists who must be removed from the political scene, the Ukrainian nationalists recalled the Lenin and Stalinist terror campaigns in return.

Around the country's frontiers stands Russia, its leader Vladimir Putin the champion of a new Russian nationalism with his own self-confidence strengthened by his intervention in Georgia and the success of the Sochi Winter Olympics. Though now weaker in military strength than in the Cold War years Moscow's view of its border peoples remains traditional, a right to intervene and the warnings of Alexander II: "Let us have no dreams."

Such was the stage setting for the events to follow the Kyiv coup.

Suggested Further Reading

Cooke, Philip and Ben H. Shepherd, *European Resistance in the Second World War,* Barnsley, Praetorian Press, 2013

Di Duca, Marc and Leonid Ragozin, *Lonely Planet Ukraine,* Kyiv, 2008

Figes, Orlando, *Revolutionary Russia, 1891-1991,* London, Penguin, 2014-06-25

Herrin, Judith, *Byzantium, The Surprising Life of a Mediaeval Empire,* London, Penguin, 2008

Lowe, Keith, Savage Continent, *Europe in the Aftermath of World War II,* New York, St Martin's Press, 2012

Riasanovsky, Nicholas V., *A History of Russia,* Oxford, Oxford University Press, 1993

Sebag Montefiore, Simon, *The Life of Potemkin,* London, Phoenix, 2001

About the Author

Dr Anthony Clayton was a lecturer at the Royal Military Academy Sandhurst from 1965 to 1993 and an Associate Lecturer at the University of Surrey from 1994 to 2008. A graduate of the University of St Andrews, he served in the colonial government of Kenya until 1963; he also served in the Territorial Army in the infantry and the Intelligence Corps, finishing as a lieutenant-colonel.

His published works include books on British and French military history, among them *The British Empire As a Superpower 1919-1939* and *The British Officer from 1660 to the Present*, *Defeat: When Nations Lose a War*; together with *France, Soldiers and Africa*, *The Wars of French Decolonization* and *Paths of Glory, the French Army 1914-1918*. For his work on the French Army he was made a Chevalier dans l'Ordre des Palmes Académiques. He has contributed chapters to several other works including *Dresden, A City Reborn*, *Volume 4 of the Oxford History of the British Empire* and the *Cambridge History of War*. His most recent work, *Warfare in Woods and Forests*, was published in 2011.

A history of the French Navy (*Three Republics, One Navy*) and a fresh biography of the controversial General Weygand (*General Weygand 1867-1965, Fortune and Misfortune*) are both expected to be published later in the autumn of 2014.

Printed in Great Britain
by Amazon